Irish Inter-Church M

Department of Theological

SALVATION AND GRACE

VERITAS

Published 1993 by
Veritas Publications
7-8 Lower Abbey Street
Dublin 1

Copyright © Irish Inter-Church Meeting, 1993

ISBN 1 85390 266 7

**British Library Cataloguing
in Publication Data.
A catalogue record for
this book is available
from the British Library.**

Cover design by Banahan McManus
Printed in the Republic of Ireland by
Paceprint Ltd, Dublin

Contents

Introduction

The world we live in is one proud of its scientific achievements, puzzled by its failures, but still confident that human beings have the capacity to strive for the better, even if slowly. Much of our world concentrates on human beings, human values and human desires. It thinks in terms of groupings and programmes to deal with and overcome the shortcomings and failures in what we have achieved up to now. On the other hand, the Christian Gospel concentrates on God as giver of salvation and grace to a sinful humanity; it speaks not primarily of progress and programme but of gift and of kingdom. It speaks of the revelation of a God who reveals himself and thus reveals human beings to themselves in faith, more than of the slow process of the discovery and analyses of science and history to show us who we are. Because of this contrast of approach the Christian churches are becoming more and more aware of the need to preach, teach and practise the Gospel of grace in a more complete and shared way. All the churches which look to Christ as their head, the Spirit of God as their life-principle and the Kingdom of God as their hope, have something important to say to the world. For this reason the following chapters are offered to promote our common witness to the Lordship of Christ in the service of saving grace. Each chapter is the result of reflection on prepared written submissions. These submissions themselves owe much to the existing inter-Church dialogues on the topics discussed. The chapters attempt to express what we hold in common and where we diverge. The hope is that these chapters will inspire further reflection at local level to help all of us in the mission of preaching, teaching and practising the Gospel. Our conviction is that we must help each other in the central tasks of our faith.

1

Basic Definitions: Salvation

1.1   The term salvation has the general meaning of peace, health, well-being, wholesomeness and deliverance from what destroys, corrupts and enslaves. Used in the Christian sense it is seen primarily in relation to a situation where we are not in a right relationship to God nor is the universe. We are subject to sin, evil, death, corruption and the powers of darkness. On the one hand, salvation is deliverance from these forces of bondage; on the other, it is being given the freedom to serve God and our world as we should, and, finally, to obtain God's gift of eternal life.

1.2   Salvation is an act that only God can perform. He has acted 'for us men and for our salvation' in Jesus Christ his Son. Christ has by his life, death and resurrection taken our sin and bondage upon himself, delivered us from the powers of sin and evil and brought us into his kingdom. This is the Gospel, the good news that is proclaimed first by Jesus himself as the Kingdom of God and then as the message of his redemption through the cross and resurrection.

1.3   This was the purpose of God from all eternity. For this reason the Father sent the Son to be the Saviour of the world and the Son came willingly by the power of the Holy Spirit. While salvation is centrally related to the Son of God incarnate, it is at the same time the will and action of the God revealed as Father, Son and Holy Spirit.

1.4   It is our Christian faith that this salvation is centred in and comes through the person and work of Christ. 'And there is salvation in no one else, for there is no other name under heaven given among men by which we must be saved' (Ac 4:12). This exclusive nature of salvation in Christ is at the same time its inclusive power, since by his coming and work he has reconciled all things in heaven and earth to himself (Col 1:20). This does not exclude the possibility that outside the walls of the Church people may know salvation.

God is free to act when, where and as he pleases. It does, however, mean that where there are signs of the kingdom in the secular world and in other religions, and people know God's love through them, this is not contrary to but confirms his action in Jesus Christ.

1.5 Since salvation comes to us through Jesus Christ alone this implies a particular view of his person – who he is. He is the one mediator between God and humankind, himself divine and human. Since only God can save and he does this in Jesus Christ the inference is that Christ is both the divine Saviour and mediator and also the human instrument of this salvation. The reality and nature of salvation imply this view of his person. 'So then, in fidelity to the Gospel and in accordance with the Scriptures, we together confess the person of Jesus Christ as the eternal son of God, who was born of the Virgin Mary and became truly man, in order to be the Saviour of the world'.[1]

2

Basic Definitions: Grace

2.1   By grace is meant the unmerited favour of God. The scriptures of the Old and New Testaments both proclaim that God has acted first and solely in our salvation, and entered into a covenant of grace with Israel fulfilled in Jesus Christ and sealed with his blood as a redemptive sacrifice.

2.2   Grace is also the term used to describe salvation as a gift. It is not due to or based on anything we have done. God has acted for the salvation of us sinners who as such deserve only his condemnation. Grace thus expresses the reality of the mercy and love of God as given to wholly undeserving sinners.

2.3   Grace is further seen as at the same time free. Nothing in God compels him so to act; he freely bestows his favour on us. Nor does anything in us make it a necessary act. While it is directed to overcome the evil in us and our world it is not conditioned by them. It is unconditional in the sense that it owes nothing to what we have been, are or may become but has its sole basis in the good will and purpose of God for our salvation.

2.4   Salvation and grace are, therefore, realities which have many aspects. It is both a past event in Christ, a present reality in faith and love, and also the object of future hope. These aspects indicate something of the depth and rich variety of meaning which point to the mystery of God's saving action for us and our world. Grace, however, comes through faith as its instrument, not its condition. Faith is, paradoxically, both God's gift and our act (Ep 2:8).

2.5   The New Testament uses many terms to describe salvation and grace in all their fullness.[2] 'Some terms are of more fundamental importance than others; but there is no controlling term or concept; they complement one another'.[3] To be true to its own sources, any theological treatment of salvation and grace is bound to draw out the riches contained in such variety.

3

Human Beings Created in God's Image

3.1 Christian revelation occupies itself with the mystery of humankind, but with humankind as understood in the light of God's self-revelation. In the words of an early Father of the Church, St Irenaeus of Lyons, 'It was not because God needed man that he first formed Adam, he was simply looking for recipients who might receive his benefits'.[4]

3.2 The Old Testament and the New Testament record of revelation emphasises two principal points in relation to the creation of humankind. These are the truths that the human person is a creature, but still a singular creature in relation to the creator and *vis-à-vis* the rest of creation.

3.3 God created humankind (Gn 2:7). This revealed truth points both to the free decision of God, as well as to the fact that the human person is a creature whose very existence is totally dependent on God's creative and sustaining power. All that we are and do, we are and do as created beings, for we are dust (Gn 3:19). This primary relationship must always be kept in mind.

3.4 We are creatures made in the image of God. This is a concept that has been interpreted in various ways. Firstly, it is regarded as humanity created for relationship with God, as a capacity for communion with the Creator.

Secondly, it is seen as human beings showing in their lives something of the character of God – knowledge, righteousness, holiness and love.

Thirdly, others see it as 'being-in-relationship', interpersonal fellowship reflecting the relationship of love and mutual self-giving between the persons of the Trinity. Each and all of these imply the goodness of the creature coming from the work of God as Creator.

3.5   These varied expressions of the image imply also an attitude of human dependence, relative freedom and genuine responsibility in relation to God. In these ways we express our creaturely being and have continual communion with God. A particular aspect of this relates to the created order for which we are given the responsibility of stewardship. This high and unique position we hold in trust from God who will require an account of our stewardship. There is thus a unique relationship between human beings as God's creatures and their environment in the rest of creation.

3.6   The Letter to the Colossians speaks of Jesus as 'the image of the unseen God' (Col 1:16). By this it means that to see him is to see the Father, to know who God is and what he is like. The image is at the same time a manifestation of God's likeness in Jesus in a life lived in unbroken fellowship with his Father. As the 'man for others', Jesus reflects in its fullness what all humans are meant to be, with and for one another in love. In this way Jesus is our example, the new and true man crowned with glory and honour – a high dignity to which, by his grace, we are also called.

3.7   The effect of sin in our human nature is that the image of God cannot be properly realised in us. It is, therefore, not only by the example of Jesus but by his grace and salvation that the image is restored and maintained. The Christian Church as the people of God is the place where this image should be best expressed and manifested and is as such the forerunner and example of what all people are meant to be.

4

The Fall

4.1 The Scriptures speak of our humanity in two ways. On the one hand it is the good creation of God, while, on the other, in an inexplicable way, it has 'fallen' away from God and is now caught up in a mesh of bondage, slavery and corruption. The Scriptures as a whole and the Genesis stories in particular give us profound insight into our human state as sinners. They show us also the consequences of this in loss of fellowship with God and of the original righteousness he intended for us by his creation.

4.2 The 'Fall' can be and is described in a great variety of ways – as pride which arrogates to itself God's prerogative and seeks to take his place; as sloth which chooses the wrong or lower way and so drags one down; as falsehood which is deceptive and rebels against the truth of God in Jesus Christ; as failure to recognise the dignity of each person; as disobedience to God's will. In the Pauline writings 'Adam' is regarded as representative man so that all humankind participates with him in a solidarity of sin. In this way all human beings share in the 'Fall', sin against God and are found to be guilty before him (Rm 5:12-19).

4.3 The consequences of the 'Fall' are far-reaching and damaging. They can be seen simply in terms of 'loss'. By the 'Fall' we lose communion with God and with one another. Some see this in terms of being disordered and damaged but not shattered and corrupted – this is more evident in the Roman Catholic tradition. Some in the Reformed tradition speak of 'total depravity' by which is not meant that we have no goodness; rather it signifies that every aspect of one's being is affected by sin.

The loss thus experienced, if left to continue, leads to permanent alienation and separation from God. This state can be described as being in the presence of God without the grace of God. It involves the condition of final damnation which, in traditional language, has been called hell.

4.4 The Scriptures and the Christian tradition speak not only of the 'Fall' of humanity; they also speak of the involvement of the rest of creation with humankind in this 'Fall' and the consequent bondage. Further, evil and evil forces are portrayed as demonic spirits that plague and influence our human nature and creation, and gain an entrance into life through our sin. We are accustomed today to think of worldly structures, political powers and other events and even persons being caught up and used by these evil powers for purposes contrary to God's will, leading to threats to human life and dignity and to the integrity of the whole of creation.

The very planet on which we live is now under threat as a result of the accelerating development of industry and technology. Science, industry and technology are goods whose benefits are beyond calculation. Still one has only to think of the pollution of the air, water and land resulting from the inordinate discharge of industrial effluent to appreciate the damage already done to our earthly home which is God's gift. The ecological movement bears tragic, eloquent witness to the fact that we have not been good stewards of the earth as God intended (Gn 1:28). This subtle presence of evil in humankind's impressive achievements is final proof of an original calamity that continues to vitiate and slant all human activity.

4.5 While sin and evil powers to a large extent dominate creation and human beings, they are only seen in all their seriousness in the light of the salvation won by Christ. He is the last Adam who has in principle overcome the power unleashed by the 'Fall'. Christ is not only the One who exposes human sin and all forms of evil but comes and saves us from their power, frees us from guilt and shame and brings us into the kingdom of his love.

In this light God sees the powers not only as our enemies but as his. However hard it may be to explain the origin of sin and evil in the world created good by God, he can never be regarded as the author of sin or evil. Rather he is the One who brings us and all things to salvation by his grace through Jesus Christ his Son, our Lord.

5

God's Saving Action in Christ

5.1 The main message of the Scriptures as a whole is God's action in coming to call and deliver Israel. God redeems humankind and creation from slavery and bondage, and brings them to himself. This begins in the Old Testament history of God's mighty acts and is completed in the person and redeeming work of Jesus Christ his Son. The Scriptures see this as recreation, showing God's will not to leave us and our world to our own sinful devices or fate, but to bring us back to himself and make us heirs of eternal life. They see creation and redemption intimately inter-related. It is through the manifestation of the children of God that creation itself is also freed from bondage to corruption (see Rm 8:19).

5.2 The New Testament underlines the costliness of this: there is no 'cheap grace' (Bonhoeffer). The Son of God became man by the will of the Father and by the Holy Spirit and took to himself our sin – became sin for us (2 Co 5:21) – bearing the judgement of God upon it on the cross and so delivering us from its guilt and power and its consequences of death, and giving us the promise and hope of eternal life. The whole New Testament focuses on Jesus Christ and especially on his death. While the cross is central, its significance is seen only in the light that the resurrection throws back on it and on the previous life of Jesus, and, as it points forward to his ascension, intercession and promised return in glory. Christ as portrayed in the whole of the New Testament, in his life, death and resurrection, ascension and intercession, is the content of our redemption. This has past, present and future significance.

One may see an aspect of this significance in the realm of creation that lies beneath the human person. Since the human being is the summit of visible creation, 'the only creature whom God has made for its own sake' (Vatican II), what happens to and in him has direct repercussions on the rest of creation. It is not surprising that the New Testament underlines the cosmic dimension of God's saving action in Christ. The Letter to the Romans portrays the whole of creation as caught up in one great groan of rebirth through the cross and glorification of Christ who is both Son of the Father and the last Adam (Rm 8:19-22).

5.3 Since the cross is the decisive event which consummates the life of Christ and accomplishes God's redemptive purpose, it is therefore central to our salvation. This is described by various metaphors in the New Testament – atonement through a blood sacrifice (cf. Lv 17:11; 1 Jn 2:2); penal suffering related to breach of the divine law and the punishment of it which Christ bears (Ga 3:13); the payment of a debt or its cancellation (Col 2:14; 1 P 1:18); warfare with evil forces and their conquest by Christ on the cross – Christus Victor (Col 1:13; 2:15); the Paschal Lamb related to the Passover Covenant (Jn 1:29; 1 Co 11:25). In the blood of Jesus the new covenant is established and a new relationship and communion with God effected. This is a completed, finished work on the cross. These metaphors and images are complementary and interweave with one another expressing in a variety of ways what God in his love has done for us and his creation in the life, death and resurrection of his Son, Jesus Christ, our Lord.

5.4 It is to be noted that, while the Church has something like a common view of the person of Christ as stated in the Ecumenical Councils of Nicaea (325), Constantinople (381) and Chalcedon (451), nothing similar has happened with the doctrine of God's redemptive work in Christ. The history of doctrine in this regard has shown varied attempts to express the mystery and meaning of God's death. Eastern christendom has seen it largely as recapitulation, that is, what was lost in Adam is restored in Christ. A further idea was that of deification where God became man that we might become god, that is, share in the divine nature (2 P 1:4). This means we have personal and corporate communion with the divine life of God, Father, Son and Holy Spirit (Rm 8:15; Ga 4:6). Yet again, some saw Christ's death as a ransom paid to the devil, a conception which has no biblical basis save that of saying that Christ paid with his life the penalty of our sin. The Middle Ages was dominated by the view of a satisfaction made by Christ to God's honour which must have our obedience and trust. Another later view of Protestant orthodoxy after the Reformation was that of penal substitution where Christ takes the place of the sinner and bears God's judgement on sin and so satisfies the divine justice.

5.5 In all these ways salvation is seen as grace, God's unmerited goodness, mercy and favour. The above outlines follow largely traditional lines and do not exclude one another but, like the New Testament metaphors, are complementary. They also point us to the mystery and depth of what God in his love has done for us in Jesus Christ. Modern scholars emphasise more the suffering of Christ on the cross, his God-forsakenness (Mk 15:34; Mt 27:46) and the need to relate this to the terrible suffering, alienation and malaise of so much of our modern life. Both in this and in the views outlined above there is a basis and a goal in the triune God. God sends the Son by the Spirit to be the Saviour of the world (Jn 3:16). The purpose of it is not only to deliver humankind and the cosmos from its perils, dangers, divisions and sinfulness, but to manifest the majesty and glory of God in the fact of Jesus Christ (Jn 1:14; 1 Co 4:6). This is seen particularly in John 17 where the death of Jesus, viewed as being lifted up on the cross, is the height of the majesty and the glory of God.

5.6 All of these views were attempts to say that God is love and that his love cannot endure sin's opposition and rejection but meets it in judgement and so in mercy. Christ the Son of God comes to set right wrong relations between God and humankind – on the one hand, to accept God's holy judgement on us in our place and, on the other hand, to overcome and destroy sin and all forms of opposition and evil. This is the work of the goodness, love and mercy of God making us righteous, that is bringing us new and right relations with God, the forgiveness of our sins and fellowship with God. It also means that, by Christ's resurrection and victory over death, we have the hope of eternal life. This saving work envisages and encompasses the whole created order and embraces it, with our humanity, in its fold. God's purpose is 'through Christ to reconcile

15

to himself all things, whether on earth or in Heaven, making peace by the blood of his cross' (Col 1:20; cf. 5:4 above). In all this, the modern emphasis on suffering, on God entering into our human situation and, indeed, identifying with us in compassion and love, and liberating us from evil, from personal sin, from structural forms of oppression, have also their proper place.

6

The Reception of Salvation and Grace through the Holy Spirit and the Church

6.1 *The Holy Spirit*

6.1.1 The Holy Spirit who is one with the Father and the Son applies to us Christ's redemption by working faith in us, uniting us with Christ and thereby bringing us into the fellowship of the Church, the body of Christ. It is our common faith that we do not become or remain Christian simply by what we do, but what Christ does for us and the Spirit applies to us. The Spirit is the Spirit of Christ who, in creating faith, unity and fellowship, maintains us in love and enables us to be witnesses to Christ in the world. At the same time the Spirit confers a great variety of gifts on his people (Charismata), distributing them variously as he wills.

6.1.2 It is also our common faith that, as the Spirit unites us with Christ, by the same act he makes us one with each other. In other words, he creates a church, the fellowship of believing people in heaven and on earth. The Church exists to be God's instrument of service in the world, building up his people in holiness and creating true and acceptable worship. It is of the greatest significance that the Apostles' Creed speaks of the holy Catholic Church within the context of faith in the Holy Spirit. It is also our view that the Church, while primarily the people of God, has also a particular form and belief structure which expresses the Gospel. To be indifferent to these (however understood) is to disrespect an important aspect of the faith.

6.1.3 Furthermore, the work of the Spirit is closely related to the Word and Sacraments, as it is to our being set right with God (justification and sanctification) and living the Christian life.

6.2 *The Nature of the Church*

6.2.1 The biblical witness relates the Church very positively to the

Gospel. It is the will of God that people should come to know God in Christ by the Holy Spirit and so be brought into a community of his people, the Church.

6.2.2 The Church is variously described in the New Testament as the People of God, the Body of Christ and the Temple of the Holy Spirit. As the People of God it is a fellowship of reconciliation, as the Body of Christ it is the community of which he is head, as the Temple of the Spirit it is where the spirit of God acts for our salvation and sends us out into the world to be witnesses to God's Grace.

6.2.3 Our traditions all lay stress on these aspects, however variously conceived. The Reformed traditions place greater emphasis on the Church as the body of those chosen and called by God with a given ministry. Roman Catholics emphasise the institution, historical continuity and the place of an ordained priesthood in the preaching of the Gospel and the celebration of the sacraments.

6.2.4 While the churches are slowly coming together and meeting with one another in greater understanding, they nonetheless hold greatly differing viewpoints on the Church and its place in the mystery of salvation. For some it is primarily the place where the Word is purely preached, the sacraments rightly celebrated but also understood as a divine-human society. For others it has a much more differentiated and graded structure, all of which is regarded as necessary for the fullness of the faith and the mystery of salvation. Both Catholics and Protestants see the Church as the *Laos*, the whole people of God. Catholics see it also as a hierarchically structured unity, giving a central role to the bishops in union with the Pope. Both Protestants and Catholics see Jesus Christ as the King and Head of the Church. Most Protestants view an earthly headship, especially one claiming to speak infallibly on faith and morals, as endangering the sole Lordship of Christ and the truth of the Gospel. Roman Catholics see the Church as linked to the Apostles and continuing the apostolic faith and sacraments through its hierarchical structure and the apostolic succession.

18

These given structures are seen as interpreting and serving the apostolic Scriptures and tradition, and as bound by them. Anglicans hold similar views, but do not accept the papacy in its present form. Many Protestants see continuity in the Church linked primarily to the Scriptures and have a structure of ministry in accord with this.

6.2.5 While in the past Protestants have sometimes tended towards an individualistic view of salvation, in more recent times greater emphasis is placed on the corporate nature of the Church. Catholics in turn have become more aware of the historical developments which moulded the papacy and, in the light of the Scriptures, are trying to understand the ministry of the Bishop of Rome in terms of the ministry of Peter in the New Testament. The chief areas of unresolved differences remaining concern Church structures, ordination, papal primacy and infallibility. Some progress is being made by situating ordination in the wider framework of 'ministry of the Gospel' and by relating Eucharist and Gospel more closely. On the very difficult and divisive questions concerning the papacy, there is agreement to differ. *Most Protestants* see the papacy as erroneous doctrine. This requires Catholics to give an account of what they believe to be both the biblical and traditional origins of the ministry of the Pope as well as of its historico-theological development. The manner in which this is done should reflect St Paul's advice 'to speak the truth in love'. What Catholics wish to affirm is that since Christ is with his Church, and since the Pope in some way represents the Church, it is fitting that he should be competent to declare and adjudicate the truth of the Gospel, with due care for the qualifications and conditions under which this happens. Protestants by contrast see the Church, by the Holy Spirit, given guidance to understand the truth of God's revelation in Scripture and to preserve the faith in its integrity without any other 'infallible' interpretation. But within the differences there is greater awareness of the need to understand one another and, as far as possible, to be reconciled to one another. However great the theological differences are, the charity of Christ pushes us forward in the ecumenical adventure of unity.

6.3 *Word and Sacraments*

6.3.1 All our churches accept that God comes and speaks to us by his Word and Sacraments. In the present understanding of the Gospel both elements are essentially related to the effective communication of the Christian message. There are nonetheless different emphases and understandings of how they are related and interpreted. The Reformation traditions accept the sixty-six books of the Old and New Testament but do not believe the Apocryphs are inspired. They also give a certain priority to the Word written and preached. They accept only two sacraments as dominical (given by the Lord), namely Baptism and the Lord's Supper.

6.3.2 Roman Catholics see Jesus Christ as the primary sacrament, the Church as primarily a sacramental reality having seven sacraments in all – baptism, eucharist, confirmation, marriage, penance, orders and the anointing of the sick. It is sometimes stated that despite our many real differences there is a basic unity in our common baptism by water in the triune name. This is true in so far as all accept this as a valid sacrament and form of baptism. However, Roman Catholics regard this as effecting the *new birth* if there is no impediment. Many Protestants and some Anglicans hold that, while baptism is a means of grace, not all who are baptised are necessarily regenerated. Here, while there is a real measure of common ground, differences of doctrinal understanding and emphasis emerge.

6.3.3 Further, both affirm that our Lord has also given us the sacrament of his body and blood in the Lord's Supper, Holy Communion or Eucharist. While many aspects are held in common and similar language used, these are sometimes given different meanings. Generally speaking the churches of the Reformation see it as a memorial of the sacrifice of Christ for our sins, a bond and pledge of our union with him and with one another. It also points forward to the End. It is made effective to us by word and spirit.

6.3.4 Roman Catholics also make these affirmations but give different interpretations to them in some respects. They see the centre and peak of all worship in the eucharistic sacrifice of the Mass. The unique sacrifice of Christ is said to be made present sacramentally in an unbloody offering of Christ to the Father. By virtue of the eucharistic action of the priest the substance of the elements is changed into the body and blood of Christ though the accidents remain the same. Transubstantiation, a 'real presence' is thus made possible through the agency of priestly consecration and the Host so set apart can be reserved, adored and exposed. These views the Reformers and their successors regarded as a form of duplication and endangering the once-for-all sacrifice of Christ. They saw worship of the Host as bordering on, if not actually, being idolatry.

6.4   *Justification and Sanctification*

6.4.1   These two doctrines emerged as central and indeed divisive at the time of the Reformation. The Reformers taught that as sinners we are accepted by God out of his sheer grace and on the basis of the righteousness of Christ, our sins are forgiven as we believe in him. We are thereby set in a process which leads to holiness (sanctification). Justification and sanctification are, according to Calvin, a twofold grace – one yet distinguishable. The sinner is *declared* righteous by God's mercy and at the same time begins to be *made* righteous. The Holy Spirit makes both possible by uniting us with Christ.

6.4.2   For Roman Catholics justification is a translation – from a state of sin to one of grace — but is not merely the forgiveness of sins. It is making a person just; it may be increased by meritorious acts or lost as a result of mortal sin. There is no clear distinction made between justification and sanctification.

6.4.3   For the Reformation tradition justification is the basis of assurance, perseverance and ultimate salvation. Roman Catholics and many Anglicans, by contrast, speak of a middle way between assurance and doubt, described by some as a moral certainty which banishes anxiety and despair!

6.4.4   One can see, therefore, that in the application of salvation, similar or identical language may and sometimes does lead to different doctrinal understandings. All agree that salvation and good works are the fruit of God's grace. Most Protestants underline strongly the sheer grace of God without human cooperation, while Roman Catholics see an element of human cooperation and merit as important. This indicates a different conception of the work of the Spirit in the Church.

6.4.5 While, therefore, both emphasise the place of the Holy Spirit, Church, ministry, Word and Sacraments and a true Christian life and vocation, the perception and interpretation of these vary.

6.4.6 As yet no real consensus has been possible though dialogue among theologians has produced some convergence today.

6.4.7 There are other important themes which have not been considered, for example, the place of Mary, the question of election, etc.

7

Conclusion

7.1 The foregoing chapters attempt to express the positions of our respective churches on the nature of salvation and grace. The chapters deal with humankind's need for reconciliation as a result of sin and the Fall, with the work of God who is 'rich in mercy' (Eph 2:4) sending his eternal son to be a sacrifice that takes our sins away (see 1 Jn 4:10), and with the communication of this gift of God (see Jn 4:10) through the Holy Spirit and in the manifold ministry of the Church. The logical sequence of these chapters already suggests the relative ease with which a large measure of agreement was reached by the members of the Department. However, the members were also well aware that the popular perception of the Faith among many Christians in all the Churches overlooks the primacy of God's love and saving grace, and tends to substitute for them an emphasis on our own efforts. This document, accordingly, has vital implications of a pastoral nature for all our Churches.

7.2 Now all this raises the whole question of how the Churches should order themselves and the lives of their members in order to hear afresh the Gospel of God's grace and witness to his trinitarian life before the men and women of our times. This decade is to be a decade of evangelisation. The document before you shows the degree to which our churches may collaborate in this task. Woe to us if we do not preach the Gospel.

7.3 The text demonstrates the depth of unity in faith among our churches on the substance of salvation. We agreed that God the Holy Trinity works our salvation, and that the resultant life of love required the paschal mystery of the Son and the gift of the Holy Spirit. We also discovered that we were unanimous in our affirmation of the necessity of the Church, of the preaching of the Gospel and of the celebration of the sacraments, in the communication of 'that life which is the light of man' (Jn 1:4).

In that way essential components of 'the faith given once for all the saints' (Jude 3) unite us and thrust us forward to pray, study and suffer for an even greater unity in the essentials. The atmosphere animating our discussions made such unity an increasingly realistic possibility.

7.4 Still, we also discovered the areas and the emphases that disunite. While the essential components are shared, they are not given equal emphasis by each Church. Besides this, certain areas of doctrine diverge. For example, chapter 6 highlights the divergent doctrine relating to the precise nature of the Church, the interrelationship of Word and Sacrament, the nature and number of the sacraments, and the exact meaning of the Church's sacramental ministry. However, even as we perceived these differences, we learned how a new language enables us to articulate our respective doctrine in such a way that we can understand one another better. Our prayer is that God will bring to perfection this good work he has begun (Ph 1:6) for his glory and for the realisation of the dying wish of our one Saviour, 'May they all be one' (Jn 17:21).

APPENDIX 1

Other Inter-Church Literature on the Subject

1. The theme of salvation and grace is central to the faith of all Christian churches. It was also central to that tremendous and dramatic struggle of the sixteenth century which we now call the Reformation and which issued in our tragic differences that collide with the explicit will of Christ (Jn 17:21f) and harm the most holy cause of proclaiming the Gospel to the whole of creation. This centrality explains the frequency with which the theme, in one form or another, has occupied centre stage in ecumenical dialogue over the past twenty years. The purpose of this appendix is to survey briefly some principal ecumenical statements which address the topic of salvation and grace.

2. In 1983, which was the fifth centenary of the birth of Martin Luther, the Catholic and Lutheran Churches in the USA produced an agreed statement called *Justification by Faith* (Augsburg Publishing House, Minneapolis, 1985). This document was in turn utilised by the ARCIC II Commission whose first production dealt with *Salvation and the Church* and which appeared only three years after the American document. 'This illustrates the interdependence of all ecumenical dialogues — an interdependence which is an expression of the growing communion which already exists between the Churches' (ARCIC II, *Salvation and the Church*, Preface).

3. The ARCIC document operates within an understanding of the Church as Koinonia. 'Koinonia with one another is entailed by our Koinonia with God in Christ. This is the mystery of the Church' (ARCIC 1, *The Final Report*, Introduction 5). This text is quoted in the very introduction of *Salvation and the Church*. In this light the Anglicans and Catholics considered the difficulties that arose between the two churches after the Reformation and consisted in the main in conflicting explanations of the manner in which divine grace related to human response. The four principal difficulties are as follows: salvation and faith (sections 9-11), salvation and justifi-

cation (12-18), salvation and good works (19-24) and, finally, salvation and the role of the Church (25-31). The document, 'an agreed statement', concludes that 'the balance and coherence of the constitutive elements of the Christian doctrine of salvation had become partially obscured in the course of history and controversy' and that 'this is not an area where any remaining differences of theological interpretation or ecclesiological emphasis, either within or between our communions, can justify our continual separation' (32). Of course, neither Church has so far endorsed the statement.

ERCDOM

4.   A third dialogue between Evangelicals and Roman Catholics is of particular interest as well. Between 1977 and 1984 the Evangelical-Roman Catholic Dialogue on Mission (ERCDOM) took place worldwide. The dialogue consisted in a sequence of three meetings which were held at Venice (1977), at Cambridge, England (1982) and at Landevennec, France (1984), when the Report was published. Unlike the ARCIC 'agreed statements', this history-making document is 'an exchange of theological views in order to increase mutual understanding and discover what theological ground they hold in common'. Its purpose, then, was not 'conceived as a step towards Church unity negotiations'.

5.   The theme of the conversations was mission, with a strong emphasis on evangelism (evangelisation). This makes the document particularly apposite for this decade of evangelism. While considering the subject of mission-evangelism the dialogue went back almost inevitably to deal with 'the Gospel of Salvation' (Section 3) and 'the response in the Holy Spirit to the Gospel' (4), as well as to 'the Church and the Gospel' (5). The dialogue on these themes, which are also vital to the whole subject of salvation and grace, shows respective positions with an encouraging clarity. The overall result is a clear vision of what is held in common, as well as a clarifying and reconciling perception of what still divides.

6.   The great subject has also been considered in a previous Ballymascanlon Report as well as in Catholic-Reformed and Catholic-Methodist dialogues.

APPENDIX 2

Exercise of the Right of Reservation

Each member of the Theology Department has a right of reservation and may request that an appendix be added summarising his disagreement. This right has been exercised below by the representative of the five smaller denominations – The Lutheran Church, The Moravian Church, The Non-Subscribing Presbyterian Church of Ireland, The Religious Society of Friends and The Salvation Army.

Salvation
Para. 1.1 The normal understanding of Salvation among all five of the smaller denominations is personal salvation at death from eternal damnation or complete annihilation. This would be expressed in teaching in terms of eternal life in either the spiritual Kingdom of God or the nearer presence of God. It should be noted that these are not alternative definitions of Salvation but alternative frames of reference within which to speak of the same reality.

Para. 1.5 All five would reject the doctrine of a Limited Atonement and teach that Salvation is open to all. Some Non-Subscribing Presbyterians argue for an ultimate universal redemption.

Grace
The views of the five on 'grace' diverge. The Lutherans and Moravians generally accept the historic forms. That is:

a. Sanctifying grace (through the sacraments)
b. Actual grace (through divine help in Christian life)
c. Prevenient (divine prompting before conversion)

The Salvation Army, Religious Society of Friends and Non-Subscribing Presbyterians would generally define 'grace' as simply the presence of God active in creating good will and spiritual help in human situations.

The Creation Myths

Para. 5.3 Many among all five, and especially among the Society of Friends and Non-Subscribing Presbyterians, would feel that the traditional arguments based on the Creation Myths as 'revealed truth' are no longer convincing in the present age, and insist that the decisive 'event' is the Incarnation – the joyful gospel that 'God is with us'.

Doctrine of the Atonement

Para. 5.4 Although the Anselmian (Penal) Doctrine of the Atonement is held among the five, the Abelardian teaching is more general, that Christ's self-sacrificing death was exemplary and inspirational.

The Sacraments

Para. 6.3 The Salvation Army and Religious Society of Friends do not celebrate sacraments as such.

Notes

1. The Evangelical Roman Catholic Dialogue on Mission, 1977-1984, p.42

2. See chapter 5, 5.

3. The Anglican Roman Church International Commission II, *Salvation and the Church,* 13.

4. *Against the Heresies*, Bk.IV, 13.

STUDY QUESTIONS

Chapter 1

1. What is the 'Christian sense' of salvation? (1.1)
2. 'Salvation is an act which only God can perform' (1.2). Why is this the case?
3. 'Salvation was the purpose of God from all eternity' (1.3). Comment.
4. Salvation in Christ is both exclusive and inclusive (1.4). Explain.
5. Show how the person and work of Christ are essential to salvation (1.5).

Chapter 2

1. Describe various meanings of the word 'grace' (2.1-3).
2. What is the relationship between grace and salvation? (2.2)
3. Describe the relationship existing between grace and faith (2.2;2.4).

Chapter 3

1. Why did God create humankind? (3.1)
2. What is the primary relationship of humankind to God? (3.3)
3. In what does the image of God in humanity consist? (3.4)
4. Jesus is 'the image of the unseen God' (Col 1:16) (3.6). Explain.
5. What restores the image of God in us? (3.7)

Chapter 4

1. Outline the two ways the Scriptures speak of our humanity (4.1).
2. What is the 'Fall'? (4.2)
3. What are the consequences of the 'Fall'? (4.3)
4. How is creation involved in the 'Fall'? (4.4)
5. 'Christ exposes human sin and all forms of evil' (4.5). Explain.

Chapter 5

1. What is the main message of the Scriptures? (5.1)
2. 'The Scriptures see creation and redemption intimately inter-related' (5.1). Comment.
3. What is the content of redemption? (5.2)
4. Describe the cosmic dimension of the redemption (5.2).
5. List the metaphors used in the New Testament to describe the redemption (5.3).
6. What emerges from the history of doctrine of the redemption? (5.4).
7. Modern scholars 'emphasise more the suffering of Christ on the cross, his God-forsakenness' (5.5). Why is this the case?
8. What is 'the basis and goal in the triune God' for the understanding of the redemption? (5.5)
9. Show how the many understandings of redemption 'were attempts to say that God is love' (5.6).
10. How does Christ's resurrection open for us the hope of eternal life? (5.6)
11. The 'modern emphasis on suffering' is part of the redemption. How? (5.5-6)
12. 'This saving work envisages and encompasses the whole created order and embraces it, with our humanity, in its fold' (5.6). Comment.

Chapter 6

1. 'The Holy Spirit who is one with the Father and the Son applies to us Christ's redemption' (6.1.1). How?
2. How do we become Christian? (6.1.1)
3. 'The Spirit creates a Church'. How? (6.1.2)
4. What is the significance of the Apostles' Creed speaking of the holy Catholic Church within the context of faith in the Holy Spirit? (6.1.2)
5. 'The biblical witness relates the Church very positively to the Gospel' (6.2.1). Comment.
6. List some of the descriptions of the Church in the New Testament (6.2.2).

7. Comment on (a) the Protestant and (b) the Catholic views of the Church's 'place in the mystery of salvation' (6.2.4).
8. Describe some of the developments in the recent understanding of the Church (6.2.5).
9. List 'the chief areas of unresolved differences' between Catholics and Protestants (6.2.5).
10. Describe the role of Word and Sacrament in the different Churches (6.3.1).
11. How much unity does our common Baptism bring about? (6.3.2)
12. How could our understandings of the Holy Eucharist be advanced? (6.3.3-4)
13. Outline the Reformation and Catholic understandings of justification and sanctification (6.4.1-4)
14. Are the differences between Protestants and Catholics on the value of good works reconcilable? (6.4.4)

Chapter 7

1. 'This document has vital implications of a pastoral nature for all our Churches' (7.1). Spell out some of those implications.

2. Has this document any significance for the work of evangelism (evangelisation)? (7.2)
3. The depth of unity in faith in relation to the message of salvation stands out. Point out the areas of agreement (7.3).
4. What are the principle areas that disunite? Do you think a still greater unity is possible? (7.4)

Appendix 1

What do you know about other inter-Church literature on salvation and grace? (1-5)